Dog's name	
Breed	
Age & Sex	
Health Issues	
Start Date	
End Date	

CHANGES / NEW DEVELOPMENTS

DATE	

CHANGES / NEW DEVELOPMENTS	
DATE	

DATE	FOOD	MEDS

POO	SKIN / GUT	OTHER

DATE	FOOD	MEDS

POO	SKIN / GUT	OTHER

DATE	FOOD	MEDS

POO	SKIN / GUT	OTHER

DATE	FOOD	MEDS

POO	SKIN / GUT	OTHER

DATE	FOOD	MEDS

POO	SKIN / GUT	OTHER

DATE	FOOD	MEDS

POO	SKIN / GUT	OTHER

DATE	FOOD	MEDS

POO	SKIN / GUT	OTHER

DATE	FOOD	MEDS

POO	SKIN / GUT	OTHER

DATE	FOOD	MEDS

POO	SKIN / GUT	OTHER

DATE	FOOD	MEDS

POO	SKIN / GUT	OTHER

DATE	FOOD	MEDS

POO	SKIN / GUT	OTHER

DATE	FOOD	MEDS

POO	SKIN / GUT	OTHER

DATE	FOOD	MEDS

POO	SKIN / GUT	OTHER

DATE	FOOD	MEDS

POO	SKIN / GUT	OTHER

DATE	FOOD	MEDS

POO	SKIN / GUT	OTHER

DATE	FOOD	MEDS

POO	SKIN / GUT	OTHER

DATE	FOOD	MEDS

POO	SKIN / GUT	OTHER

DATE	FOOD	MEDS

POO	SKIN / GUT	OTHER

DATE	FOOD	MEDS

POO	SKIN / GUT	OTHER

DATE	FOOD	MEDS

POO	SKIN / GUT	OTHER

DATE	FOOD	MEDS

POO	SKIN / GUT	OTHER

DATE	FOOD	MEDS

POO	SKIN / GUT	OTHER

DATE	FOOD	MEDS

POO	SKIN / GUT	OTHER

DATE	FOOD	MEDS

POO	SKIN / GUT	OTHER

DATE	FOOD	MEDS

POO	SKIN / GUT	OTHER

DATE	FOOD	MEDS

POO	SKIN / GUT	OTHER

DATE	FOOD	MEDS

POO	SKIN / GUT	OTHER

DATE	FOOD	MEDS

POO	SKIN / GUT	OTHER

Notes

Printed in Poland
by Amazon Fulfillment
Poland Sp. z o.o., Wrocław